A Place of Quiet Rest

JOURNAL

"NOTHING CAN COMPARE TO THE JOY
AND PRIVILEGE OF SITTING AND LEARNING
AT THE FEET OF OUR HEAVENLY FATHER."

Nancy DeMoss Wolgemuth

MOODY PUBLISHERS
CHICAGO

© 2005, 2025 by
REVIVED HEARTS FOUNDATION

All rights reserved. No part of this book may be reproduced in any form without permission in writing from the publisher, except in the case of brief quotations embodied in critical articles or reviews.

Interior design: Kaylee Lockenour Dunn
Cover design: Brittany Schrock
Cover design of floral pattern copyright © 2025 by IchdaAlimul/Adobe Stock (737664346). All rights reserved.
Author photo: Nathan Bollinger

ISBN: 978-0-8024-3809-6

Originally delivered by fleets of horse-drawn wagons, the affordable paperbacks from D. L. Moody's publishing house resourced the church and served everyday people. Now, after more than 125 years of publishing and ministry, Moody Publishers' mission remains the same—even if our delivery systems have changed a bit. For more information on other books (and resources) created from a biblical perspective, go to www.moodypublishers.com or write to:

Moody Publishers
820 N. LaSalle Boulevard
Chicago, IL 60610

1 3 5 7 9 10 8 6 4 2

Printed in Colombia

From My Heart to Yours

I've often said that if I could share just one message, it would be on the value and importance of a personal devotional life.

For sure, there are other vital truths that need to be communicated—I've addressed many of these over the course of decades of ministry. But I've always believed that the most helpful thing I could do for the women I serve is to get them into Scripture for themselves. That's because I'm convinced that if you and I are consistently getting to know God and His ways through His Word, He will show us everything we need to know in order to deal with our most thorny, perplexing problems and to live godly, fruitful, blessed lives.

That conviction is what motivated me to write my first book, *A Place of Quiet Rest*. And what a great joy it has been in the twenty-five years since its initial release, to see how the Lord has used this message to draw readers into a more vibrant relationship with Him.

A 30-Day Challenge

Over the years, I've been encouraged to discover how hungry many believers are for a more consistent, meaningful devotional life. But I've also seen that most people feel overwhelmed with their existing schedule. Or they're just not sure how to get started—they need a jump start to help them develop the habit of carving out time in their day to spend alone with the Lord.

One of the most practical means I have found to accomplish that goal is a simple 30-Day Challenge. Rather than asking people to make a lifetime commitment to have a daily quiet time (a lofty aspiration, but one they may not keep for long), I've challenged them to begin by making a commitment to *spend some time alone with God in His Word and in prayer, every day, for the next thirty days.*

I've extended this challenge to thousands of women and have been thrilled to see how God has used it to make a world of difference in the lives of tired, needy believers who want to know God in a more intimate way. Here are some of the kinds of comments I've received from those who have taken the 30-Day Challenge:

A truly phenomenal experience . . .

My life has been beautifully transformed . . .

When I started, 15 minutes seemed too long, but now two hours isn't long enough! . . .

It's been more than 30 days, and I don't want to stop! . . .

I've been revived! . . .

The whole idea of a daily devotional life may be new to you. Or perhaps you've started—and quit—and started again, only to quit again—maybe many times. Or you may already be enjoying a consistent time alone with God each day. Wherever you are, I want to encourage you to go further . . . to press deeper into an intimate relationship with God.

Over the years, whenever I've spoken on the devotional life, I've closed my message by asking this question: "How many of you would be honest enough to admit that you do *not* currently have a consistent personal devotional life?" I've asked this question scores of times—with groups of lay people, Bible study leaders, and full-time Christian workers. And invariably, 80 to 90 percent of those in the room raise their hand, acknowledging that they are not currently having a regular quiet time.

I have followed that question by inviting people to take the 30-Day Challenge. What a joy it has been to see many thousands of people stand to their feet, signifying their commitment to *spend some time alone with the Lord each day—for the next thirty days.*

A Personal Invitation

If you've not been enjoying a consistent devotional time with the Lord, the 30-Day Challenge may be just the place for you to start—or to get started again.

You may wonder how you can possibly add "one more thing" to your already over-crowded schedule. Let me assure you that if you will make knowing God your number one priority, He will show you how to fit everything into your day that is on *His* "to-do" list for you.

Setting aside time alone with the Lord each day has become an absolute necessity for me; there is no richer blessing in my life. That doesn't mean it's always easy—in fact, virtually every day I deal with distractions, excuses, and misplaced priorities that would keep me from the "one thing" that matters most (Psalm 27:4). But I've determined that this is a battle worth waging, because I know I cannot be the woman God made me to be—nor can *you*—apart from time spent each day in His presence.

This journal is your invitation to take the first step. Are you ready to get started? If so, I'd encourage you to sign on the next page as an expression of your commitment to the Lord.

> **By God's grace, out of a desire to know Him more intimately, I purpose to spend some time alone with the Lord in the Word and in prayer, every day for the next thirty days.**
>
> Signed _____
>
> Date _____

Once you've made this commitment, expect that some days you may not have the desire to keep it. Remember that as you choose to feed your soul, your spiritual hunger will grow. Some days you may not seem to be able to find the time to follow through. But if you miss a day, *don't give up!* Simply determine by God's grace to press on. Also, consider reaching out to a friend letting them know that you have committed to this step in developing a daily devotional time and ask that they pray for you. Telling someone else about your commitment can help provide additional accountability and encouragement to see it through.

My prayer is that the 30-Day Challenge will become a lifelong pattern and priority of seeking the Lord every day for the rest of your life, and that your life will bear the sweet fruit of an every-growing love relationship with Him.

Seeking Him with you,

How to Use This Journal

The purpose of this resource is to help you develop a more intimate and consistent relationship with the Lord. As was the practice of Jesus, as well as biblical characters like Moses, Joshua, David, and Daniel, I would encourage you, if possible, to meet God early in the day—while it is relatively quiet and your mind is free from distractions. Whatever the time of day, find a solitary place and make sure you have your Bible and a journal of some sort, whether digital or simple paper and pen.

I have found that my time with the Lord is generally more meaningful (and my mind less prone to wander) when I record what God shows me in my time with Him. These pages are designed to facilitate that process.

The journal is divided into thirty days, each of which includes a quote from my book *A Place of Quiet Rest*, as well as the following elements:

Preparing My Heart

Take time to quiet your heart before the Lord and focus your mind on Him. Ask Him to speak to you. Let Him know that you are ready to listen to Him, to learn from Him, and to respond to whatever He says to you through His Word.

Listening to God

Read and meditate on a passage in the Word of God. (If you don't currently have a Bible reading plan, you may want to use the 30-day plan suggested on page 9 of this journal.) Ask the Holy Spirit to illuminate the Scriptures to your understanding and apply it to your life. As you read, look for the following:

Observations—*What does this passage say?* Record observations about your Scripture reading. Summarize or paraphrase the passage. Identify key facts, themes, or characters.

Interpretation—*What does this passage mean?* What does this passage reveal about God and His ways, about man, about Christ, about salvation, about the Christian life, etc.? Are there any promises to claim, commands to obey, examples to follow, or sins to avoid?

Application—***What should I do?*** In light of what God has revealed, how should you respond? What changes need to be made in your life? How can this passage be practically applied to your life?[1]

Responding to God

A helpful tool for responding to God in praise and prayer is the simple acrostic A-C-T-S:

Adoration—Worship God for who He is. Focus on one or more of His attributes (holiness, mercy, majesty, omnipotence, etc.) that are revealed in His Word.

Confession—Agree with God about anything He has revealed in your life that is not pleasing to Him. Receive the forgiveness that He has provided through the sacrifice of Christ on the cross.

Thanksgiving—Thank God for what He has done, for His gifts, and for how He has spoken to you through His Word.

Supplication—Bring your requests to Him, both for your own needs and for the needs of others (intercession). Ask Him for grace to obey His Word.

Remember, this journal is intended to be a tool; don't get hung up on the mechanics. The goal is not to fill in every line or even to write something in every section. The point is to get into the Word and get the Word into you.

Keep in mind that it's not enough to just read your Bible (important as that is). The object is that the words that are printed on the page would become written on your heart, and that you would come to know God intimately and reflect His heart and ways to others.

---

1. Chapter 9 of *A Place of Quiet Rest*—"Getting the Word into You"—expands on how to look for observations, interpretation, and applications, and includes additional suggestions for how to read and study the Bible. Chapters 10 and 11 of *A Place of Quiet Rest* have more helpful insights on how to respond to God through praise and prayer.

Suggested Scripture Readings

If you don't already have a Scripture reading plan, here's one you may want to use for the next thirty days. The journey through the gospel of Mark will give you a fresh glimpse of the Savior and His redemptive life and ministry. Reading three of Paul's epistles will help you understand how to live as a redeemed child of God.

- **Day 1:** Mark 1
- **Day 2:** Mark 2
- **Day 3:** Mark 3
- **Day 4:** Mark 4
- **Day 5:** Mark 5
- **Day 6:** Mark 6
- **Day 7:** Mark 7
- **Day 8:** Mark 8
- **Day 9:** Mark 9
- **Day 10:** Mark 10
- **Day 11:** Mark 11
- **Day 12:** Mark 12
- **Day 13:** Mark 13
- **Day 14:** Mark 14
- **Day 15:** Mark 15
- **Day 16:** Mark 16
- **Day 17:** Ephesians 1
- **Day 18:** Ephesians 2
- **Day 19:** Ephesians 3
- **Day 20:** Ephesians 4
- **Day 21:** Ephesians 5
- **Day 22:** Ephesians 6
- **Day 23:** Philippians 1
- **Day 24:** Philippians 2
- **Day 25:** Philippians 3
- **Day 26:** Philippians 4
- **Day 27:** Colossians 1
- **Day 28:** Colossians 2
- **Day 29:** Colossians 3
- **Day 30:** Colossians 4

DATE: _____

Day 1

"I MUST MAKE A DELIBERATE,
DAILY CHOICE TO SIT AT HIS FEET,
LISTEN TO HIS WORD,
RECEIVE HIS LOVE,
AND LET HIM CHANGE ME."

PREPARING MY HEART

As you begin, take a moment to quiet your heart before the Lord and focus on Him. Ask Him to speak to you. Let Him know that you are willing to listen and learn from Him through His Word.

LISTENING TO GOD

Scripture Passage: _____

OBSERVATIONS: What does this passage say?

_____

_____

_____

_____

_____

_____

_____

INTERPRETATION: What does it mean?

APPLICATION: What should I do?

RESPONDING TO GOD

Adoration

Confession

Thanksgiving

Supplication

TAKEAWAY THOUGHT:

What key verse or insight will you take with you into your day?

DATE: _____

Day 2

"DEVELOPING INTIMACY WITH THE LORD REQUIRES A CONSCIOUS, DELIBERATE CHOICE TO PUT HIM FIRST, ABOVE ANYTHING AND EVERYTHING ELSE IN OUR BUSY LIVES."

PREPARING MY HEART

As you begin, take a moment to quiet your heart before the Lord and focus on Him. Ask Him to speak to you. Let Him know that you are willing to listen and learn from Him through His Word.

LISTENING TO GOD

Scripture Passage: _____

OBSERVATIONS: What does this passage say?

_____
_____
_____
_____
_____
_____
_____

INTERPRETATION: What does it mean?

APPLICATION: What should I do?

RESPONDING TO GOD

Adoration

Confession

Thanksgiving

Supplication

TAKEAWAY THOUGHT:

What key verse or insight will you take with you into your day?

DATE: _____

Day 3

"IN THE SCRIPTURES WE ENCOUNTER
A GOD WHO MOVES TOWARD US,
SEEKS TO DRAW US TO HIMSELF,
KNOWS US INTIMATELY,
AND INVITES US TO KNOW HIM."

PREPARING MY HEART

As you begin, take a moment to quiet your heart before the Lord and focus on Him. Ask Him to speak to you. Let Him know that you are willing to listen and learn from Him through His Word.

LISTENING TO GOD

Scripture Passage: _____

OBSERVATIONS: What does this passage say?

_____
_____
_____
_____
_____
_____
_____
_____

INTERPRETATION: What does it mean?

APPLICATION: What should I do?

RESPONDING TO GOD

Adoration

Confession

Thanksgiving

Supplication

TAKEAWAY THOUGHT:

What key verse or insight will you take with you into your day?

DATE: _____

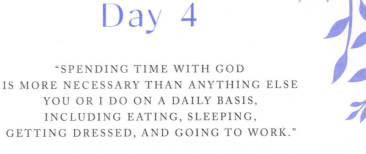

Day 4

"SPENDING TIME WITH GOD
IS MORE NECESSARY THAN ANYTHING ELSE
YOU OR I DO ON A DAILY BASIS,
INCLUDING EATING, SLEEPING,
GETTING DRESSED, AND GOING TO WORK."

PREPARING MY HEART

As you begin, take a moment to quiet your heart before the Lord and focus on Him. Ask Him to speak to you. Let Him know that you are willing to listen and learn from Him through His Word.

LISTENING TO GOD

Scripture Passage: _____

OBSERVATIONS: What does this passage say?

_____
_____
_____
_____
_____
_____
_____
_____
_____

INTERPRETATION: What does it mean?

APPLICATION: What should I do?

RESPONDING TO GOD

Adoration

Confession

Thanksgiving

Supplication

___

TAKEAWAY THOUGHT:

What key verse or insight will you take with you into your day?

___

DATE: _____

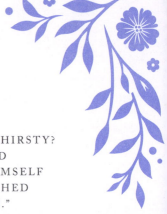

Day 5

"ARE YOU SPIRITUALLY DRY AND THIRSTY?
BEGIN TO PRAISE THE LORD
AND HE WILL FILL YOU WITH HIMSELF
UNTIL YOUR THIRST IS QUENCHED
AND YOUR CUP OVERFLOWS."

PREPARING MY HEART

As you begin, take a moment to quiet your heart before the Lord and focus on Him. Ask Him to speak to you. Let Him know that you are willing to listen and learn from Him through His Word.

LISTENING TO GOD

Scripture Passage: _____

OBSERVATIONS: What does this passage say?

_____
_____
_____
_____
_____
_____
_____

INTERPRETATION: What does it mean?

APPLICATION: What should I do?

RESPONDING TO GOD

Adoration

Confession

Thanksgiving

Supplication

TAKEAWAY THOUGHT:

What key verse or insight will you take with you into your day?

DATE: _____

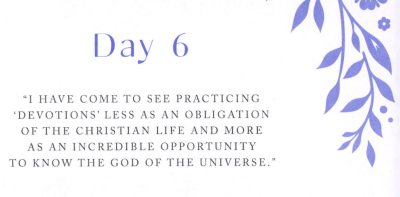

Day 6

"I HAVE COME TO SEE PRACTICING
'DEVOTIONS' LESS AS AN OBLIGATION
OF THE CHRISTIAN LIFE AND MORE
AS AN INCREDIBLE OPPORTUNITY
TO KNOW THE GOD OF THE UNIVERSE."

PREPARING MY HEART

As you begin, take a moment to quiet your heart before the Lord and focus on Him. Ask Him to speak to you. Let Him know that you are willing to listen and learn from Him through His Word.

LISTENING TO GOD

Scripture Passage: _____

OBSERVATIONS: What does this passage say?

_____
_____
_____
_____
_____
_____
_____
_____

INTERPRETATION: What does it mean?

APPLICATION: What should I do?

RESPONDING TO GOD

Adoration

Confession

Thanksgiving

Supplication

TAKEAWAY THOUGHT:

What key verse or insight will you take with you into your day?

DATE: _____

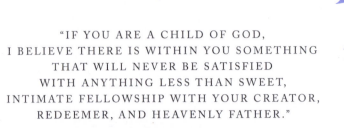

Day 7

"IF YOU ARE A CHILD OF GOD,
I BELIEVE THERE IS WITHIN YOU SOMETHING
THAT WILL NEVER BE SATISFIED
WITH ANYTHING LESS THAN SWEET,
INTIMATE FELLOWSHIP WITH YOUR CREATOR,
REDEEMER, AND HEAVENLY FATHER."

PREPARING MY HEART

As you begin, take a moment to quiet your heart before the Lord and focus on Him. Ask Him to speak to you. Let Him know that you are willing to listen and learn from Him through His Word.

LISTENING TO GOD

Scripture Passage: _____

OBSERVATIONS: What does this passage say?

_____
_____
_____
_____
_____
_____
_____

INTERPRETATION: What does it mean?

APPLICATION: What should I do?

RESPONDING TO GOD

Adoration

Confession

Thanksgiving

Supplication

TAKEAWAY THOUGHT:

What key verse or insight will you take with you into your day?

DATE: _____

Day 8

"HE HAS ISSUED TO YOU AND ME
AN INVITATION TO DRAW NEAR TO HIM
AND EXPERIENCE
AN INTIMATE LOVE RELATIONSHIP
WITH HIM."

PREPARING MY HEART

As you begin, take a moment to quiet your heart before the Lord and focus on Him. Ask Him to speak to you. Let Him know that you are willing to listen and learn from Him through His Word.

LISTENING TO GOD

Scripture Passage: _____

OBSERVATIONS: What does this passage say?

_____
_____
_____
_____
_____
_____
_____

INTERPRETATION: What does it mean?

APPLICATION: What should I do?

RESPONDING TO GOD

Adoration

Confession

Thanksgiving

Supplication

TAKEAWAY THOUGHT:

What key verse or insight will you take with you into your day?

DATE: _____

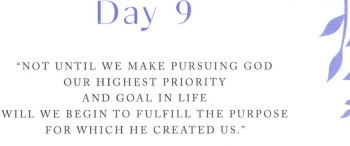

Day 9

"NOT UNTIL WE MAKE PURSUING GOD
OUR HIGHEST PRIORITY
AND GOAL IN LIFE
WILL WE BEGIN TO FULFILL THE PURPOSE
FOR WHICH HE CREATED US."

PREPARING MY HEART

As you begin, take a moment to quiet your heart before the Lord and focus on Him. Ask Him to speak to you. Let Him know that you are willing to listen and learn from Him through His Word.

LISTENING TO GOD

Scripture Passage: _____

OBSERVATIONS: What does this passage say?

_____
_____
_____
_____
_____
_____
_____
_____

INTERPRETATION: What does it mean?

APPLICATION: What should I do?

RESPONDING TO GOD

Adoration

Confession

Thanksgiving

Supplication

___

TAKEAWAY THOUGHT:

What key verse or insight will you take with you into your day?

___

DATE: _____

Day 10

"GOD NEVER INTENDED
THAT WE SHOULD MERELY
GET INTO HIS WORD.
HIS INTENT HAS ALWAYS BEEN THAT
THE WORD SHOULD GET INTO US."

PREPARING MY HEART

As you begin, take a moment to quiet your heart before the Lord and focus on Him. Ask Him to speak to you. Let Him know that you are willing to listen and learn from Him through His Word.

LISTENING TO GOD

Scripture Passage: _____

OBSERVATIONS: What does this passage say?

INTERPRETATION: What does it mean?

APPLICATION: What should I do?

RESPONDING TO GOD

Adoration

Confession

Thanksgiving

Supplication

TAKEAWAY THOUGHT:

What key verse or insight will you take with you into your day?

DATE: _____

Day 11

"THE ETERNAL GOD AND CREATOR
OF THE UNIVERSE—THE ONE WHO
MEASURES THE SPAN OF THE UNIVERSE
WITH THE WIDTH OF HIS HAND—
THAT GOD HAS SPOKEN TO US, HIS FINITE
BUT INFINITELY LOVED CREATURES."

PREPARING MY HEART

As you begin, take a moment to quiet your heart before the Lord and focus on Him. Ask Him to speak to you. Let Him know that you are willing to listen and learn from Him through His Word.

LISTENING TO GOD

Scripture Passage: _____

OBSERVATIONS: What does this passage say?

_____
_____
_____
_____
_____
_____
_____

INTERPRETATION: What does it mean?

APPLICATION: What should I do?

RESPONDING TO GOD

Adoration

Confession

Thanksgiving

Supplication

TAKEAWAY THOUGHT:

What key verse or insight will you take with you into your day?

DATE: _____

Day 12

"FOR JESUS, TIME ALONE WITH GOD
WAS ESSENTIAL.
IT WAS HIS LIFELINE TO THE FATHER,
THE HIGHEST PRIORITY
OF HIS LIFE."

PREPARING MY HEART

As you begin, take a moment to quiet your heart before the Lord and focus on Him. Ask Him to speak to you. Let Him know that you are willing to listen and learn from Him through His Word.

LISTENING TO GOD

Scripture Passage: _____

OBSERVATIONS: What does this passage say?

_____
_____
_____
_____
_____
_____
_____
_____

INTERPRETATION: What does it mean?

APPLICATION: What should I do?

RESPONDING TO GOD

Adoration

Confession

Thanksgiving

Supplication

TAKEAWAY THOUGHT:

What key verse or insight will you take with you into your day?

DATE: _____

Day 13

"DURING OUR QUIET TIME
WE ENTER INTO HIS PRESENCE
AND LAY OUR LIVES BEFORE HIM.
THEN, WITH HIS WORD OPEN BEFORE US,
WE LISTEN AND SEEK TO DISCOVER
HIS HEART ON THE ISSUE."

PREPARING MY HEART

As you begin, take a moment to quiet your heart before the Lord and focus on Him. Ask Him to speak to you. Let Him know that you are willing to listen and learn from Him through His Word.

LISTENING TO GOD

Scripture Passage: _____

OBSERVATIONS: What does this passage say?

_____

_____

_____

_____

_____

_____

_____

INTERPRETATION: What does it mean?

APPLICATION: What should I do?

RESPONDING TO GOD

Adoration

Confession

Thanksgiving

Supplication

TAKEAWAY THOUGHT:

What key verse or insight will you take with you into your day?

DATE: _____

Day 14

"AS PART OF A COMMUNITY OF FAITH, WE NEED TIMES TO WORSHIP, PRAY, AND SEEK THE LORD IN THE COMPANY OF GOD'S PEOPLE. BUT WE MUST ALSO HAVE TIMES THAT ARE SET APART TO BE ALONE WITH HIM."

PREPARING MY HEART

As you begin, take a moment to quiet your heart before the Lord and focus on Him. Ask Him to speak to you. Let Him know that you are willing to listen and learn from Him through His Word.

LISTENING TO GOD

Scripture Passage: _____

OBSERVATIONS: What does this passage say?

_____
_____
_____
_____
_____
_____
_____
_____

INTERPRETATION: What does it mean?

APPLICATION: What should I do?

RESPONDING TO GOD

Adoration

Confession

Thanksgiving

Supplication

TAKEAWAY THOUGHT:

What key verse or insight will you take with you into your day?

DATE: _____

Day 15

"OUR MERCIFUL, LONG-SUFFERING
HEAVENLY FATHER
NEVER STOPS PURSUING
A LOVE RELATIONSHIP
WITH HIS CHILDREN."

PREPARING MY HEART

As you begin, take a moment to quiet your heart before the Lord and focus on Him. Ask Him to speak to you. Let Him know that you are willing to listen and learn from Him through His Word.

LISTENING TO GOD

Scripture Passage: _____

OBSERVATIONS: What does this passage say?

_____
_____
_____
_____
_____
_____
_____
_____

INTERPRETATION: What does it mean?

APPLICATION: What should I do?

RESPONDING TO GOD

Adoration

Confession

Thanksgiving

Supplication

TAKEAWAY THOUGHT:

What key verse or insight will you take with you into your day?

DATE: _____

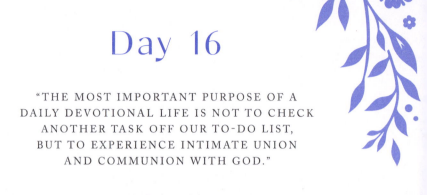

Day 16

> "THE MOST IMPORTANT PURPOSE OF A
> DAILY DEVOTIONAL LIFE IS NOT TO CHECK
> ANOTHER TASK OFF OUR TO-DO LIST,
> BUT TO EXPERIENCE INTIMATE UNION
> AND COMMUNION WITH GOD."

PREPARING MY HEART

As you begin, take a moment to quiet your heart before the Lord and focus on Him. Ask Him to speak to you. Let Him know that you are willing to listen and learn from Him through His Word.

LISTENING TO GOD

Scripture Passage: _____

OBSERVATIONS: What does this passage say?

_____
_____
_____
_____
_____
_____
_____

INTERPRETATION: What does it mean?

APPLICATION: What should I do?

RESPONDING TO GOD

Adoration

Confession

Thanksgiving

Supplication

___

TAKEAWAY THOUGHT:

What key verse or insight will you take with you into your day?

___

DATE: _____

Day 17

"I'VE COME TO BELIEVE THAT
IT'S IMPOSSIBLE FOR ME TO CULTIVATE
AN INTIMATE RELATIONSHIP WITH GOD
OR TO BECOME THE WOMAN HE WANTS ME TO BE
APART FROM SPENDING DAILY TIME
ALONE WITH HIM."

PREPARING MY HEART

As you begin, take a moment to quiet your heart before the Lord and focus on Him. Ask Him to speak to you. Let Him know that you are willing to listen and learn from Him through His Word.

LISTENING TO GOD

Scripture Passage: _____

OBSERVATIONS: What does this passage say?

_____
_____
_____
_____
_____
_____
_____

INTERPRETATION: What does it mean?

APPLICATION: What should I do?

RESPONDING TO GOD

Adoration

Confession

Thanksgiving

Supplication

TAKEAWAY THOUGHT:

What key verse or insight will you take with you into your day?

DATE: _____

Day 18

"THERE SIMPLY IS
NO SUBSTITUTE FOR
SPENDING CONSISTENT,
QUALITY TIME ALONE
IN HIS PRESENCE."

PREPARING MY HEART

As you begin, take a moment to quiet your heart before the Lord and focus on Him. Ask Him to speak to you. Let Him know that you are willing to listen and learn from Him through His Word.

LISTENING TO GOD

Scripture Passage: _____

OBSERVATIONS: What does this passage say?

INTERPRETATION: What does it mean?

APPLICATION: What should I do?

RESPONDING TO GOD

Adoration

Confession

Thanksgiving

Supplication

TAKEAWAY THOUGHT:

What key verse or insight will you take with you into your day?

DATE: _____

Day 19

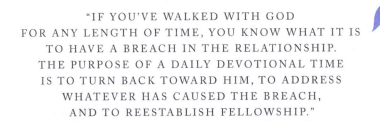

"IF YOU'VE WALKED WITH GOD
FOR ANY LENGTH OF TIME, YOU KNOW WHAT IT IS
TO HAVE A BREACH IN THE RELATIONSHIP.
THE PURPOSE OF A DAILY DEVOTIONAL TIME
IS TO TURN BACK TOWARD HIM, TO ADDRESS
WHATEVER HAS CAUSED THE BREACH,
AND TO REESTABLISH FELLOWSHIP."

PREPARING MY HEART

As you begin, take a moment to quiet your heart before the Lord and focus on Him. Ask Him to speak to you. Let Him know that you are willing to listen and learn from Him through His Word.

LISTENING TO GOD

Scripture Passage: _____

OBSERVATIONS: What does this passage say?

_____
_____
_____
_____
_____
_____
_____
_____

INTERPRETATION: What does it mean?

APPLICATION: What should I do?

RESPONDING TO GOD

Adoration

Confession

Thanksgiving

Supplication

TAKEAWAY THOUGHT:

What key verse or insight will you take with you into your day?

DATE: _____

Day 20

"NOTHING CAN COMPARE
TO THE JOY AND PRIVILEGE
OF SITTING AND LEARNING
AT THE FEET OF
OUR HEAVENLY FATHER."

PREPARING MY HEART

As you begin, take a moment to quiet your heart before the Lord and focus on Him. Ask Him to speak to you. Let Him know that you are willing to listen and learn from Him through His Word.

LISTENING TO GOD

Scripture Passage: _____

OBSERVATIONS: What does this passage say?

_____
_____
_____
_____
_____
_____
_____
_____

INTERPRETATION: What does it mean?

APPLICATION: What should I do?

RESPONDING TO GOD

Adoration

Confession

Thanksgiving

Supplication

TAKEAWAY THOUGHT:

What key verse or insight will you take with you into your day?

DATE: _____

Day 21

"AS HIS SPIRIT WORKS WITHIN US,
OUR SPIRITS BECOME PLIABLE
AND ARE BROUGHT INTO SUBMISSION
TO HIS AUTHORITY,
AND WE JOYOUSLY EMBRACE HIS WILL."

PREPARING MY HEART

As you begin, take a moment to quiet your heart before the Lord and focus on Him. Ask Him to speak to you. Let Him know that you are willing to listen and learn from Him through His Word.

LISTENING TO GOD

Scripture Passage: _____

OBSERVATIONS: What does this passage say?

_____
_____
_____
_____
_____
_____
_____
_____

INTERPRETATION: What does it mean?

APPLICATION: What should I do?

RESPONDING TO GOD

Adoration

Confession

Thanksgiving

Supplication

TAKEAWAY THOUGHT:

What key verse or insight will you take with you into your day?

DATE: _____

Day 22

*"GOD DESIRES TO HAVE
THE KIND OF RELATIONSHIP
WITH US WHERE
WE ARE QUICK TO SEEK
HIS COUNSEL."*

PREPARING MY HEART

As you begin, take a moment to quiet your heart before the Lord and focus on Him. Ask Him to speak to you. Let Him know that you are willing to listen and learn from Him through His Word.

LISTENING TO GOD

Scripture Passage: _____

OBSERVATIONS: What does this passage say?

_____

_____

_____

_____

_____

_____

_____

_____

INTERPRETATION: What does it mean?

APPLICATION: What should I do?

RESPONDING TO GOD

Adoration

Confession

Thanksgiving

Supplication

TAKEAWAY THOUGHT:

What key verse or insight will you take with you into your day?

DATE: _____

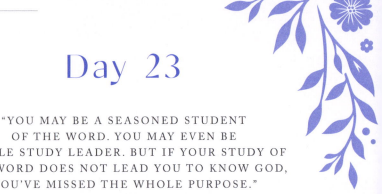

Day 23

"YOU MAY BE A SEASONED STUDENT
OF THE WORD. YOU MAY EVEN BE
A BIBLE STUDY LEADER. BUT IF YOUR STUDY OF
THE WORD DOES NOT LEAD YOU TO KNOW GOD,
YOU'VE MISSED THE WHOLE PURPOSE."

PREPARING MY HEART

As you begin, take a moment to quiet your heart before the Lord and focus on Him. Ask Him to speak to you. Let Him know that you are willing to listen and learn from Him through His Word.

LISTENING TO GOD

Scripture Passage: _____

OBSERVATIONS: What does this passage say?

_____
_____
_____
_____
_____
_____
_____
_____

INTERPRETATION: What does it mean?

APPLICATION: What should I do?

RESPONDING TO GOD

Adoration

Confession

Thanksgiving

Supplication

TAKEAWAY THOUGHT:

What key verse or insight will you take with you into your day?

DATE: _____

Day 24

*"DAY AFTER DAY, AS I SOAK IN HIS WORD
AND OPEN UP MY HEART
TO THE WORK OF HIS SPIRIT,
HE IS FAITHFUL TO BRING TO MY ATTENTION
THINGS THAT HAVE GRIEVED HIM."*

PREPARING MY HEART

As you begin, take a moment to quiet your heart before the Lord and focus on Him. Ask Him to speak to you. Let Him know that you are willing to listen and learn from Him through His Word.

LISTENING TO GOD

Scripture Passage: _____

OBSERVATIONS: What does this passage say?

_____
_____
_____
_____
_____
_____
_____

INTERPRETATION: What does it mean?

APPLICATION: What should I do?

RESPONDING TO GOD

Adoration

Confession

Thanksgiving

Supplication

TAKEAWAY THOUGHT:

What key verse or insight will you take with you into your day?

DATE: _____

Day 25

"AS YOU SPEND TIME EACH DAY
BEHOLDING JESUS IN HIS WORD
AND LISTENING TO HIS VOICE,
YOUR LIFE WILL BE TRANSFORMED
FROM THE INSIDE OUT."

PREPARING MY HEART

As you begin, take a moment to quiet your heart before the Lord and focus on Him. Ask Him to speak to you. Let Him know that you are willing to listen and learn from Him through His Word.

LISTENING TO GOD

Scripture Passage: _____

OBSERVATIONS: What does this passage say?

_____
_____
_____
_____
_____
_____
_____
_____

INTERPRETATION: What does it mean?

APPLICATION: What should I do?

RESPONDING TO GOD

Adoration

Confession

Thanksgiving

Supplication

_____

TAKEAWAY THOUGHT:

What key verse or insight will you take with you into your day?

_____

DATE: _____

Day 26

"IF WE FAIL TO STOP AND DRAW
FROM HIS FRESH, INFINITE SUPPLY
OF MERCY AND GRACE, WE'LL FIND OURSELVES
HAVING TO OPERATE OUT OF
OUR OWN MEAGER RESOURCES."

PREPARING MY HEART

As you begin, take a moment to quiet your heart before the Lord and focus on Him. Ask Him to speak to you. Let Him know that you are willing to listen and learn from Him through His Word.

LISTENING TO GOD

Scripture Passage: _____

OBSERVATIONS: What does this passage say?

_____
_____
_____
_____
_____
_____
_____

INTERPRETATION: What does it mean?

APPLICATION: What should I do?

RESPONDING TO GOD

Adoration

Confession

Thanksgiving

Supplication

TAKEAWAY THOUGHT:

What key verse or insight will you take with you into your day?

DATE: _____

Day 27

"IN THAT DAILY TIME ALONE WITH HIM,
HE CALMS MY SPIRIT, SLOWS DOWN
MY RACING PULSE, AND GIVES ME FRESH
PERSPECTIVE AND RENEWED DESIRE AND
STRENGTH TO SERVE HIM FOR ANOTHER DAY."

PREPARING MY HEART

As you begin, take a moment to quiet your heart before the Lord and focus on Him. Ask Him to speak to you. Let Him know that you are willing to listen and learn from Him through His Word.

LISTENING TO GOD

Scripture Passage: _____

OBSERVATIONS: What does this passage say?

_____
_____
_____
_____
_____
_____
_____
_____

INTERPRETATION: What does it mean?

APPLICATION: What should I do?

RESPONDING TO GOD

Adoration

Confession

Thanksgiving

Supplication

TAKEAWAY THOUGHT:

What key verse or insight will you take with you into your day?

DATE: _____

Day 28

"KNOWING THE TENDENCY OF MY HEART
TO WANT ITS OWN WILL,
I HAVE MADE IT A FREQUENT PRACTICE
TO GET ON MY KNEES BEFORE THE LORD.
IN DOING SO, I ACKNOWLEDGE THAT
HE IS MY LORD AND I AM HIS SERVANT."

PREPARING MY HEART

As you begin, take a moment to quiet your heart before the Lord and focus on Him. Ask Him to speak to you. Let Him know that you are willing to listen and learn from Him through His Word.

LISTENING TO GOD

Scripture Passage: _____

OBSERVATIONS: What does this passage say?

_____
_____
_____
_____
_____
_____
_____

INTERPRETATION: What does it mean?

APPLICATION: What should I do?

RESPONDING TO GOD

Adoration

Confession

Thanksgiving

Supplication

TAKEAWAY THOUGHT:

What key verse or insight will you take with you into your day?

DATE: _____

Day 29

"TIME SPENT ALONE
WITH JESUS EACH DAY
WILL ORDER OUR HEARTS
AND GRANT A SENSE
OF DIRECTION."

PREPARING MY HEART

As you begin, take a moment to quiet your heart before the Lord and focus on Him. Ask Him to speak to you. Let Him know that you are willing to listen and learn from Him through His Word.

LISTENING TO GOD

Scripture Passage: _____

OBSERVATIONS: What does this passage say?

_____
_____
_____
_____
_____
_____
_____
_____

INTERPRETATION: What does it mean?

APPLICATION: What should I do?

RESPONDING TO GOD

Adoration

Confession

Thanksgiving

Supplication

___

TAKEAWAY THOUGHT:

What key verse or insight will you take with you into your day?

DATE: _____

Day 30

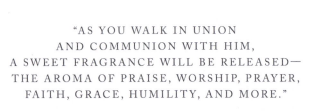

*"AS YOU WALK IN UNION
AND COMMUNION WITH HIM,
A SWEET FRAGRANCE WILL BE RELEASED—
THE AROMA OF PRAISE, WORSHIP, PRAYER,
FAITH, GRACE, HUMILITY, AND MORE."*

PREPARING MY HEART

As you begin, take a moment to quiet your heart before the Lord and focus on Him. Ask Him to speak to you. Let Him know that you are willing to listen and learn from Him through His Word.

LISTENING TO GOD

Scripture Passage: _____

OBSERVATIONS: What does this passage say?

_____

_____

_____

_____

_____

_____

_____

_____

INTERPRETATION: What does it mean?

APPLICATION: What should I do?

RESPONDING TO GOD

Adoration

Confession

Thanksgiving

Supplication

TAKEAWAY THOUGHT:

What key verse or insight will you take with you into your day?

Nancy DeMoss Wolgemuth is the founder and lead Bible teacher for *Revive Our Hearts*, a ministry dedicated to calling women to freedom, fullness, and fruitfulness in Christ. Nancy's love for Christ and passion for helping women cultivate a vibrant daily devotional life are evident through her writing, digital, and conference outreaches and her two daily audio teachings—*Revive Our Hearts* and *Seeking Him*. Her books have sold millions of copies and are reaching the hearts of women around the world. Nancy and her husband, Robert, live in Michigan.

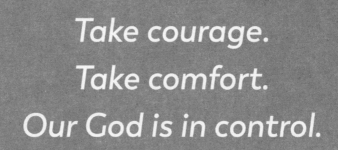

"The God of heaven rules. He rules over every tide of history, over every king and kingdom, over every activity we undertake, over every person and part of His Creation."

—Nancy DeMoss Wolgemuth

He will meet you there.

A daily devotional time will forever change your relationship with Jesus.

A Place of Quiet Rest offers practical advice, encouragement, and tools to seek after God for a lifetime.

Calling Women to Freedom,
Fullness, and Fruitfulness in Christ

Daily Teaching | Events | Broadcast Media

Resources | Digital Content

For additional teaching from Nancy DeMoss Wolgemuth visit
ReviveOurHearts.com
Your Trustworthy Source for Biblical Truth